Mad Isn't Bad

A Child's Book About Anger

Written by
Michaelene Mundy

Illustrated by
R. W. Alley

ABBey PRess
Publications
St. Meinrad, IN 47577

For my husband, Linus,
and our three children—
Em, Mike, and Pat—
all four of whom I have been mad at
and who have been mad at me...
and I still love them a whole bunch!

Text © 1999 Michaelene Mundy
Illustrations © 1999 St. Meinrad Archabbey
Published by Abbey Press Publications
1 Hill Drive
St. Meinrad, Indiana 47577

Library of Congress Catalog Number
99072094

ISBN 978-0-87029-331-3

Printed in the United States of America.

A Message to Parents, Teachers, and Other Caring Adults

Everyone gets angry; it's part of our human makeup. We get angry at events, at objects, at people we know, people we don't know, and even (especially?) people we love. Even infants show anger. There is a baby's cry that is clearly recognizable as anger, rather than distress or sadness.

When we were little, many of us were taught not to show our anger—or even to talk about it. Some adults in our lives went so far as to say that anger is bad. But anger isn't bad. It's what we do with anger that can be good or bad for ourselves and those around us.

Children often do not realize they can make choices when they're angry or upset. They may feel their only option is to do and say angry things—angrily! We adults, too, sometimes fail to realize that we can make choices rather than "lose our cool" in the heat of anger. But as we humans, large and small, grow in maturity, we come to understand that anger can be dealt with, coped with, and expressed—in very healthy and life-giving ways.

As you already know, the best way to help a child learn healthy ways of coping is to model good coping skills ourselves. What a gift we offer children when we show them that we can channel the energy of anger to make constructive changes and get positive results. We can teach them the benefit of talking it out, rather than slugging it out; the value of creative, assertive confrontation; the helpfulness of physical outlets for frustration; the value of letting go and forgiving.

Anger is a given in life, a definite part of the range of human emotions we all experience. Through this book, I hope that we can communicate to young people positive and peaceful ways of handling anger, as we live these ways ourselves.

—*Michaelene Mundy*

Mad Isn't Bad

Feelings like happiness and sadness, fear and anger are all part of being alive and being you. Go ahead and feel your feelings. It's good to be you!

You might think it's bad to be angry, but that's not true. It's normal to feel angry when you think you are not being treated fairly. It's how you show your anger that can sometimes be a problem for you or those around you.

Mad Can Even Be Good

Anger is like fire. Fire is good when it keeps us warm and helps us cook food. But fire can sometimes get out of control.

Anger can be good when it makes you want to do something about a bad situation. It can give you energy to work harder to solve a problem or to get that project right. When your team is losing a game, anger can put more power behind that swing or kick. Anger can help you to tell someone what's bothering you, so you can work together to work things out.

What Makes You Mad?

Sometimes you may think you have to be perfect. You might get angry when you can't do something as well as someone older.

People may do or say things that make you angry, even though they might not know they're hurting you.

Sometimes you might feel frustrated when you can't fix a problem or change a bad situation. And sometimes things just go wrong. It's not anybody's fault.

It helps to know exactly what you're mad at. You might be mean to the cat because you really are still mad at the kid who was mean to you at recess.

What Does "Mad" Feel Like?

Anger can make you feel like you're going to explode. Your face feels hot, you breathe faster, and your heart beats faster. Your hands want to grab, hit, or throw something, and your feet want to kick or run. Your voice wants to yell or cry.

Anger gives you energy. Try to think of some safe ways to use that energy without hurting yourself, others, or other people's things.

Why You Need to Let Out Your Anger

Unless you let out your anger in a safe way, you may just keep blaming someone else or yourself—and stay mad. This doesn't feel good and gets you nowhere with the problem.

Anger can be "catching." If you get mad and throw something or hit someone, the other person might get angry, too. You'll end up feeling worse instead of better.

But if you can find good ways to let out the energy of anger, you'll feel better. You might even find yourself laughing later at what you must have looked or sounded like!

You Can CHOOSE What to Do

Anger can be scary when you don't know how to handle it. But you can make choices about what to do with your anger. You can yell and throw a fit—or you can stay calm. If you are able to stay calm, you will be able to act in a fairer and smarter way.

When something makes you angry, you don't have to do something about it right then. Stop and count to ten (or 100!) and THINK about the best thing to do or say.

It's natural to want to blame someone else for making you angry. But YOU are the one who's angry, and YOU are the one who can do something about it. Think about what made you mad. Ask yourself what you can do to feel better.

When You're Mad, SAY So!

Say, "I'm angry" or "I'm mad." It's important to realize you are angry and to let others know. But try to say it without screaming or whining.

Talk with the person who made you angry. Tell him or her how you feel and why. Say, "I am mad because _____ ." Tell the other person what you need. For example, you might say calmly to your sister: "I'd like to use the computer, too. What about a half hour for me after you have a half hour?"

Let people know when you're even "a little" angry. Otherwise, you may end up waiting until you are "a lot" angry. Then your anger is harder to control.

Good Ways to Let Out Anger

You want to find good, safe ways to express anger—ways that don't harm others or yourself, and don't cause you to regret later what you said or did.

Punch a pillow or stomp on packing bubbles. Or run around outside. Or find a place to scream at the top of your lungs. (You might want to ask an adult where a safe place would be to do these things.)

Take a "time out" from what's making you angry. Go to a quiet place—maybe out on the swing or under a tree. Or talk to someone about how you feel.

Not-So-Good Ways to Let Out Anger

Don't destroy something when you're angry—your own things or someone else's. You'll probably regret it later when you've calmed down, and then it may be hard to fix the damage.

When we're angry, we can hurt people as much by what we say as by what we do. We can hurt their feelings. Angry words hurt as much as hitting.

More Good Ways to Handle Anger

Take a deep breath and then let it out slowly. You'll find you don't feel so angry and can think more clearly. (You might have to do this more than once.)

Sometimes you might need to practice a skill you want to be better at, so it won't be so frustrating. If you're mad at a new game, you may need to go over the instructions or ask for help. Do something different for a while. Rest quietly or play a game you already know.

It may help to write a note to let someone know what's bothering you. Or draw a picture of how you feel and share it with someone who cares about you.

Get Help From Caring Adults

Think about people you love—your parents, grandparents, aunts, uncles, an older brother or sister. How do they handle their anger in safe ways? Ask them about good ways to deal with anger.

Things that aren't important to you cannot make you angry. Let others know what's important to you. People who care about you want to help.

If you see yourself getting angry a lot, talk to someone about it. Is something going on in your life that you feel bad about?

Being Mad at God

Did you know it's okay to be mad even at God? Go ahead and tell God about the way you feel. God can take it!

Praying is another great way to ask for help in dealing with anger. God loves you and wants you to feel good.

God knows, too, that not everything in life is fair. Bad things do happen to good people. And it's okay to be mad when that happens. The important thing is to try to be fair to others whenever you can.

When People Are Angry at YOU

When someone gets angry with you, listen to the reasons. Listening is important because it helps you understand the other person's side.

You may need to ask someone why he or she is angry. You can help others to see that they're angry and to think about the best way to handle it.

Forgiving Others— and Yourself

If you hurt someone or break something in anger, say, "I'm sorry." Promise yourself to do better the next time. God forgives you. Forgive yourself.

Just because you or someone else is angry doesn't mean you don't still love each other. You might need to say or hear, "I love you." Then talk with each other about why you are angry.

Everybody gets angry sometimes. It's okay to be mad. It's the way you handle your anger that makes all the difference.

Michaelene Mundy holds degrees in elementary education, as well as graduate degrees in school and community counseling. She has taught third and fourth graders, worked with learning-disabled children, and has served as a counselor on the college level. The mother of three children, she now works as a high school guidance counselor. She is also the author of the Elf-help Book for Kids *Sad Isn't Bad: A Good-Grief Guidebook for Kids Dealing With Loss.*

R. W. Alley is the illustrator for the popular Abbey Press adult series of Elf-help books, as well as an illustrator and writer of children's books. He lives in Barrington, Rhode Island, with his wife, daughter, and son. See a wide variety of his works at: www.rwalley.com.